www.castlepointbooks.com

The Castle Point Books trademark is owned by Castle Point Publishing, LLC.
Castle Point books are published and distributed by St. Martin's Publishing Group.

ISBN 978-1-250-34008-5 (paper over board)
ISBN 978-1-250-34009-2 (ebook)

Design by Joanna Williams
Editorial by Monica Sweeney

Images used under license by Shutterstock.com

Our books may be purchased in bulk for promotional, educational,
or business use. Please contact your local bookseller or the
Macmillan Corporate and Premium Sales Department at 1-800-221-7945,
extension 5442, or by email at MacmillanSpecialMarkets@macmillan.com.

First Edition: 2024

10 9 8 7 6 5 4 3 2 1

MOCKTAIL LOUNGE

CREATIVE **ALCOHOL-FREE COCKTAILS**
To ELEVATE YOUR SIPPING HOUR

DYLAN SWIFT

CASTLE POINT BOOKS
NEW YORK

Contents

IT'S MOCKTAIL HOUR! 1

CHAPTER 1
A Little Something Sunshine 3
Spritzes, citrus, and bubbles in your cup

CHAPTER 2
Wind-Down Hour 33
Bevvies with soothing components
for that after-work reward

CHAPTER 3
Oh This? It's a Mocktail! 61
Alcohol-free concoctions with wow-factor

CHAPTER 4
Icy Blends & Sweet Treats 91
Flavorful frozen mocktails
and dessert drinks

INDEX 120

IT'S MOCKTAIL HOUR!

Welcome to your very own *Mocktail Lounge,* where enjoying alcohol-free beverages doesn't mean you have to skimp on style, fun, or flavor. Gone are the days of mocktails being the killjoy of the party, when the only options available were syrupy sweet or just plain boring. Here, you can toast to whatever you want with a glass you're excited to clink. Whether you enjoy something to sip after a long day, while out with friends or coworkers, or in the middle of a big celebration, you can do it with a zero-proof bevvy in hand.

As you get cozy in this particular lounge, you'll notice a couple of things. Each chapter has its own special twist to help you decide what kind of mocktail mood you're in. "A Little Something Sunshine" is for when you're feeling spritzy. These drinks focus on bubbly potions that feel light and easy to drink. "Wind-Down Hour" is made up of relaxing concoctions, many of which shine best with nonalcoholic wine or adaptogen-based mixers that will give you a little calming glow. "Oh This? It's a Mocktail!" is your not-so-subtle opportunity to show off drinks with pizzazz—the kind that alcohol-based drinks always take credit for. "Icy Blends & Sweet Treats" are those dessert-hour or any-hour blends that will satisfy your sweet tooth in liquid form.

The best part of the mocktail revolution is that skipping alcohol has never been easier or more fun—whether that means you're doing Dry January, looking for ways to reduce your alcohol intake to feel healthier, or you and alcohol just aren't a thing at all. With *Mocktail Lounge,* you can look forward to the sound of a cork popping, enjoy the feeling of stemware in your hand as you swirl something beautiful, and savor the sip of a drink without worry. So mix up something sober and get back to the party!

CHAPTER 1

A LITTLE SOMETHING SUNSHINE

Honeydew-Aloe Cooler..........4

Orange Spritz 7

Sunlit Café Tónica.................8

Summer in Italy Spritz........11

Kiwi Summer Water 12

Lavender Cape Codder.......15

Apricot Seltzer 16

Strawberry Water 19

Apple Mimosa 20

Pomegranate Spritzer 23

Watermelon Mojito 24

Pineapple Sour 27

Lemon Sparkler 28

Blood-Orange Zester 31

HONEYDEW-ALOE COOLER

Ooh! This drink will give you chills, and it's not even frozen. A delightful blend of soothing honeydew and cucumber paired with hydrating coconut and aloe vera, this mocktail is as healthy as it is fun. Let it be your spa day in a glass.

Makes 1 mocktail

- ¼ cup chopped cucumber
- ¼ cup chopped honeydew melon
- ½ ounce lime juice
- 2 ounces aloe vera juice
- 4 ounces coconut water
- 1 aloe leaf
- 1 cucumber wheel

In a cocktail shaker, muddle the cucumber, honeydew melon, and lime juice. Add the aloe vera juice, coconut water, and ice to the shaker. Shake vigorously for one minute and strain into a wineglass with ice. Garnish this cooling bevvy with an aloe leaf and cucumber wheel to make it sing.

Bevs with Benefits

Aloe, you amazing nectar, you! Aloe vera juice contains antioxidants, vitamin C, calcium, and beta-carotene—among other goodies. Drinking a small amount of aloe vera juice per day can hydrate your skin for a clearer complexion and boost immune function. It also helps with digestion, so don't go overboard.

ORANGE SPRITZ

Give your brunch-side companion a little love. With a splash of alcohol-free liqueur, this mocktail is nothing but the bright side. If you prefer a drink that's a little less sweet, just reduce the amount of orange juice and add more soda water for a refreshing zing.

Makes 1 mocktail

- 1½ ounces nonalcoholic Campari liqueur
- 4 ounces fresh orange juice
- Splash soda water
- 1 orange wedge
- 1 rosemary sprig

In a glass filled with ice, combine the nonalcoholic Campari liqueur, orange juice, and soda water. Garnish with the orange wedge and rosemary, and let the citrus spruce up your day.

SUNLIT CAFÉ TÓNICA

A mocktail for your brunching hour, the Sunlit Café Tónica is a zesty and refreshing cooler that will give you a little boost of energy while letting you toast to easy mornings with friends. This surprising combination of bubbles, citrus, and espresso is *everything*.

Makes 1 mocktail

- **4 ounces quality tonic water**
- **2 ounces chilled espresso**
- **Spritz of lemon**
- **1 lemon wheel**

In a large glass filled with ice, combine the tonic water and espresso. Spritz the drink with lemon, garnish with the lemon wheel, and sip away the morning.

SUMMER IN ITALY SPRITZ

Spritz, spritz, honey. Summer's most refreshing bevvy just got a glow up. You don't have to fake it with a sugary mix of not-from-concentrate juices. You can find alcohol-free replacements that will make this mocktail taste just as good as an Aperol Spritz but leave you feeling light and refreshed.

Makes 1 mocktail

- 3 ounces nonalcoholic Italian spritz liqueur
- 2 ounces nonalcoholic prosecco
- 1 dash nonalcoholic bitters
- Splash sparkling water
- 1 orange slice

In a stemmed glass filled with ice, combine the non-alcoholic Italian spritz liqueur, nonalcoholic prosecco, nonalcoholic bitters, and sparkling water. Garnish with the orange slice and drift off on your favorite pool floatie.

KIWI SUMMER WATER

Welcome to paradise in a glass. This tropical concoction has the tart flavors of blueberry and kiwi to perk you up, and the soothing aroma of rosemary to calm you down. You can make the most of this winning flavor combo by replacing regular simple syrup with a rosemary-infused version.

Makes 1 mocktail

- 1 kiwi, peeled and sliced, divided
- ½ cup blueberries, divided
- Juice of ½ lime
- ½ ounce simple syrup
- 6 ounces soda water
- 1 rosemary sprig

In a tall glass, muddle half of the kiwi, half of the blueberries, and lime juice. Add ice to the mixture and stir in the simple syrup and soda water. Garnish this tart treat with the remaining kiwi slices, blueberries, and rosemary sprig.

LAVENDER CAPE CODDER

Let's not overcomplicate things. The Lavender Cape Codder lets little Miss Cranberry do her thing with a fun lavender accent. Take a peek at Mocktail Magic (page 24) for details on how to make your own lavender simple syrup.

Makes 1 mocktail

- **4 ounces cranberry juice**
- **½ ounce lavender simple syrup**
- **½ ounce lemon juice**
- **1 lavender sprig**
- **2 lemon wheels**

In a glass filled with ice, combine the cranberry juice, lavender simple syrup, and lemon juice. Garnish with the lavender sprig and lemon wheels, and transport yourself to the seaside.

APRICOT SELTZER

Purposefully reserved, this drink is light on apricot nectar and big on bubbles. Light, refreshing, and just a zip of fruit flavor, this Apricot Seltzer is a reviving blend you'll feel good about. And who doesn't love a drink that comes with fun little snacks?

Makes 1 mocktail

- ½ ounce apricot nectar
- 4 ounces soda water
- Spritz of lemon
- 1 apricot, pitted and sliced
- 1 thyme sprig

In a glass filled with ice, combine the apricot nectar and soda water. Spritz the drink with a lemon and stir in the apricot slices. Garnish with thyme for a stunning presentation.

 BEVS WITH BENEFITS

There is such a thing as a mocktail hangover. Keep your sugary alcohol replacements in check by mixing up elevated elixirs that are mostly water. Fruits like apricots are hydrating and full of fiber, which promotes healthy skin and good digestion.

STRAWBERRY WATER

If you've never found yourself dreaming away in the middle of a strawberry patch (perhaps on the set of your very own rom-com), here is your opportunity. This gentle mixture of nature's sweetest treat and just a touch of rose water makes Strawberry Water as aromatic as it is pleasing.

Makes 1 mocktail

- **4 ounces strawberry juice**
- **⅛ teaspoon rose water**
- **Splash water**
- **Spritz of lemon**
- **2–3 strawberry slices**
- **2 lemon wheels**

In a glass filled with ice, combine the strawberry juice, rose water, and water. Spritz the drink with a lemon and stir in the strawberry and lemon garnishes.

MOCKTAIL MAGIC ✦

Some juices are hard to find. To make your own strawberry juice, simply toss a healthy handful of fresh strawberries (stems removed) into a blender with a cup of water and blend until smooth. Squeeze the mixture through cheesecloth to remove the pulp and get your fresh juice. Spritzes of citrus or dashes of sweetener can help bring out the strawberry flavor depending on what your batch needs.

APPLE MIMOSA

Mimosas aren't all brunch and orange juice. This breezy beauty is a crisp fall day in a glass. If you can't find apple cider or it's not in season, go for cold-pressed or unfiltered apple juice. Toast to something or nothing at all with this easy and satisfying sipper.

Makes 1 mocktail

- 2½ ounces apple cider
- 2½ ounces nonalcoholic sparkling wine
- 1 apple slice, like Granny Smith

In a champagne flute, combine the apple cider and the nonalcoholic sparkling wine. Garnish with an apple slice and drift off to autumnal bliss.

POMEGRANATE SPRITZER

Tart up your mocktail hour with the best of the best: pomegranate and lemon. The sparkling water smooths out the bite and the itty-bitty smidge of pomegranate syrup softens the mixture with just a touch of sweetness. Enjoy this zippy pick-me-up when you want something bright and refreshing.

Makes 1 mocktail

- 4 ounces sparkling water
- 1 tablespoon pomegranate syrup
- 1 ounce lemon juice
- ¼ cup pomegranate arils
- 2 lemon wheels
- 1 rosemary sprig

In a glass filled with ice, combine the sparkling water, pomegranate syrup, lemon juice, pomegranate arils, and lemon wheels. Garnish with the rosemary sprig for a wisp of wintertime.

WATERMELON MOJITO

Get that summer feeling with a Watermelon Mojito. The easy version of this liquid beauty calls for pre-prepared, pulp-free watermelon juice. But if you love the texture of one of nature's prettiest fruits, feel free to blend 1 cup of watermelon cubes with the lime juice and simple syrup, then strain.

Makes 1 mocktail

- 2–3 chilled watermelon cubes
- 5 ounces watermelon juice
- 1 ounce lime juice
- ½ ounce mint simple syrup
- 2 lime wheels
- Splash lime seltzer
- 1–2 mint sprigs
- 1 flower sprig

In a highball glass with a mix of ice and watermelon cubes, combine the watermelon juice, lime juice, simple syrup and lime wheels. Add a splash of lime seltzer and garnish with the mint and flower sprigs.

MOCKTAIL MAGIC ✦

You can stir up your own simple syrup by heating equal parts water and sugar, maple syrup, agave, or honey. Pop in an infusion like mint, lavender, rosemary, jalapeño, rhubarb, fruit, or food-grade flowers. All you need is a few sprigs or slices. When the sweetener has dissolved, let the mixture cool and strain out any solids. *Et voilà*, you're a mixologist.

PINEAPPLE SOUR

Who needs a piña colada when a Pineapple Sour is just the thing? This fizzy tropical potion gets its texture from the egg white and its hype from being amazing. Kick back and enjoy the closest hammock with a mocktail that captures all the best parts of a tropical vacation without the sunburns and regrets.

Makes 1 mocktail

- **4 ounces pineapple juice**
- **1 ounce lemon juice**
- **1 egg white**
- **½ ounce coconut cream**
- **½ ounce ginger syrup**
- **1 pineapple slice**

In a cocktail shaker filled with ice, combine the pineapple juice, lemon juice, egg white, coconut cream, and ginger syrup. Shake vigorously for one minute and strain into a coupe glass. Garnish with the pineapple to complete your perfect match.

LEMON SPARKLER

Brighten your day with this citrus stunner! This gorgeous elixir is just sweet enough to bring you a little joy, but not so sweet that you end up feeling sluggish. The Lemon Sparkler is the perfect refresher for when you need a little minty pick-me-up.

Makes 1 mocktail

- **Juice of 1 lemon**
- **1 ounce mint simple syrup**
- **6 ounces soda water**
- **2 lemon wheels**
- **1 mint sprig**

In a large glass filled with ice, combine the lemon juice, mint simple syrup, and soda water. Garnish your sparkling concoction with the lemon wheels and add a little zip with the mint leaves.

BLOOD ORANGE ZESTER

Level up your wine hour with the Blood Orange Zester. This crisp and cool blend of nonalcoholic dry white wine, like a Sauvignon Blanc, with the gorgeous pep of blood orange seltzer makes this one wine spritzer you'll want to savor.

Makes 1 mocktail

- 4 ounces nonalcoholic dry white wine
- Splash blood orange seltzer
- 2 blood orange slices
- 1 rosemary sprig

In a cocktail glass filled with ice, combine the nonalcoholic white wine and blood orange seltzer. Garnish with the orange slices and rosemary—then toast to your good choices!

CHAPTER 2

WIND-DOWN HOUR

Rose Water Garden Party.................. 34

Fig Lemonade..................... 37

Chamomile-Citrus Relaxer 38

Pomegranate Glimmer....... 41

Golden Berry Spritzer 42

Pear & Cinnamon Sparkler................................. 45

Orange Mojito.................. 46

Hibiscus Iced Tea.............. 49

Raspberry Seltzer.............. 50

Sparkling Negroni............. 53

Never Better Iced Tea........54

Pretty in Purple Martini 57

Orange-Thyme Detox........ 58

ROSE WATER GARDEN PARTY

It's your very own rose garden in a glass. You don't need that much rose flavoring to start feeling rosie, and the best alcohol-free spirits to choose will be clear and herbal, like a gin. The Rose Water Garden Party is subtle, lovely, and whisks you away to paradise with its floral scent.

Makes 1 mocktail

- 1 ounce rose syrup or ¼ teaspoon rose water and 1 ounce simple syrup
- 1 ounce nonalcoholic spirit
- 2 ounces soda water
- Spritz of lime
- 1 mint sprig

In a cocktail glass filled with ice, combine the rose syrup, nonalcoholic spirit, and soda water. Spritz it with lime and top with mint before gliding off into a secret garden.

🍷 Bevs with Benefits

Rose water has been used medicinally for ages, but it's the aroma that can be your biggest boost when you include it in your zero-proof potions. Rose water notes swirling around your senses can reduce tension, ease headaches, and calm the mind.

FIG LEMONADE

Congratulations to the fig for its recent rebrand. This long-neglected fruit is often associated with cookies someone's grandma buys, and it's about time for it to shine. If you include a nonalcoholic spirit, choose one reminiscent of gin or vodka. This melding of fig and almond flavors in a softly sweet lemonade is truly something special.

Makes 1 mocktail

- 1 ounce lemon juice
- 1 fig, sliced in half
- 1 ounce nonalcoholic spirit
- ½ ounce orgeat syrup
- 4 ounces water
- 2 fig slices
- 1 basil sprig

In a cocktail shaker, muddle the lemon juice and the fig. Add ice to the mixture and stir in the nonalcoholic spirit, orgeat syrup, and water. Shake and strain into a wineglass. Garnish with the fig slices and basil before kicking your feet up.

CHAMOMILE-CITRUS RELAXER

Mellow out in style. A step up from evening tea, this Chamomile-Citrus Relaxer is a cooling and calming way to slip into serenity. If it's wintertime and you're looking for something warm, you can turn this into a toddy by swapping out the ice and seltzer for a nonalcoholic whiskey.

Makes 1 mocktail

- 1 chamomile tea bag
- ½ cup boiling water
- 2 ounces lemon juice
- ¾ ounce simple syrup
- Splash seltzer
- 1 lemon slice
- 1–2 flower sprigs

Steep the chamomile tea in the boiling water for five minutes. Remove the tea bag and let the liquid cool. In a cocktail shaker filled with ice, combine the chamomile tea, lemon juice, and simple syrup. Shake and strain into a glass, and then top with seltzer. Garnish with the lemon slice and flower sprig before twirling in a meadow.

🍷 *Bevs with Benefits*

What can't chamomile do? An ancient medicine that seems to have it all figured out, chamomile is a healing flower that soothes the skin, settles the stomach, and relaxes the mind. Chamomile tea can help calm your nerves for better sleep and quell nausea and other gastrointestinal discomforts.

POMEGRANATE GLIMMER

Oh, she pretty. Give yourself some positive affirmations with the Pomegranate Glimmer. Effervescent, beautiful, and appropriately tart, this bubbly blend of flavors is just the right tonic to remind you of everything that's going right.

Makes 1 mocktail

• 1 ounce pomegranate juice
• 1½ ounces nonalcoholic spirit
• Splash soda water or nonalcoholic sparkling wine
• 2–3 pomegranate arils
• Microgreens

In a cocktail shaker filled with ice, combine the pomegranate juice, nonalcoholic spirit, and soda water. Stir and strain into a coupe glass filled with ice. Garnish with the pomegranate arils and microgreens for a playful pop of color.

GOLDEN BERRY SPRITZER

Whoever invented the white wine spritzer was not wrong. Is it a poor excuse for a drink that aunts of the 1980s guzzled with abandon, or is it refreshing, hydrating, and economical? The Golden Berry Spritzer is an ode to these ladies, highlighted by the mix of an adaptogen-infused sparkling aperitif and the sweet and sharp little golden fruit.

Makes 1 mocktail

- 2 golden berries
- ½ ounce simple syrup
- 1 ounce water
- 4 ounces nonalcoholic sparkling white wine or aperitif

In a cocktail shaker, muddle 1 golden berry, husk removed, with the simple syrup and the water. Shake and strain into a cocktail glass filled with ice and top with the nonalcoholic sparkling aperitif. Garnish with the remaining golden berry and sip back to relax.

BEVS WITH BENEFITS

Choose a nonalcoholic aperitif with adaptogens like lemon balm and L-theanine. Lemon balm helps reduce stress and can increase libido, while L-theanine is an amino acid that sharpens the mind.

PEAR & CINNAMON SPARKLER

It's an autumnal rom-com in here. The Pear & Cinnamon Sparkler has all of the notes of a made-for-streaming movie with the lovely but underappreciated pear, herbs probably plucked from a family farm, and an entire cinnamon stick that shows the true meaning of togetherness. This gorgeous drink is heartwarming and reviving all at once.

Makes 1 mocktail

- 1 ounce pear juice
- ½ ounce simple syrup
- 3 ounces soda water
- 1 cinnamon stick
- 1 pear slice
- 1 thyme sprig

In a cocktail glass filled with ice, combine the pear juice, simple syrup, and soda water. Swirl the cinnamon stick in the glass several times to bring out the cinnamon flavor. Garnish with the pear slice and thyme to pretty up your drinking hour.

BEVS WITH BENEFITS

Set the mood with a sprinkle of adaptogen powders. Popular brands offer formulas containing mood-regulating adaptogens like reishi mushroom, which strengthens your immune system and can help settle stress. Use as directed and enrich your mocktail with these blends for a gentle way to smooth your mood.

ORANGE MOJITO

Give orange juice the space to be bigger than a mimosa. The poster child for vitamin C gets to shine in this Orange Mojito, which balances the brightness of the citrus with cooling mint. Combined with a nonalcoholic orange liqueur, this drink gives happy hour a whole new vibe.

Makes 1 mocktail

- 3–4 lime wedges
- 2 mint sprigs
- 1 ounce nonalcoholic orange liqueur
- 2 ounces fresh orange juice
- Splash soda water
- 1 orange twist

In a cocktail shaker, muddle the lime and 1 mint sprig. Add the orange liqueur, orange juice, and ice to the mixture. Shake and strain into a large glass with ice and top with soda water. Garnish with the orange twist and the remaining mint for something a little zippy.

HIBISCUS ICED TEA

This drink is a seaside breeze in a glass. With this simple iced tea that leaves room for playfulness (add your zero-proof spirit of choice, why don't you?), there's something special about letting hibiscus do its thing. If you prefer loose-leaf hibiscus, steep 1–2 tablespoons depending on your desired strength.

Makes 1 mocktail

- 1 hibiscus flower tea bag
- 1 cup boiling water
- ½ ounce simple syrup
- Lemon wheels

Steep the hibiscus tea in the boiling water for five minutes. Remove the tea bag and refrigerate the liquid to cool completely. In a large glass filled with ice, combine the hibiscus tea, simple syrup, and lemon wheels for a tropical tea time.

🍷 BEVS WITH BENEFITS

Hibiscus is here for you. A gorgeous flower in your hair and so much more, hibiscus is known to reduce inflammation, lower blood pressure, and support liver function.

RASPBERRY SELTZER

We love a drink that comes with snacks. This Raspberry Seltzer is a celebration of the beloved berry. The accompanying flavors lift the raspberries up rather than compete, and you are encouraged to stir in enough whole berries so you can have a little treat to glam up the aesthetic.

Makes 1 mocktail

- 2 lime wedges
- 2 mint sprigs
- ½ cup raspberries, divided
- 2 ounces nonalcoholic white wine
- 1 ounce lime juice
- ½ ounce simple syrup
- Splash seltzer

In a large glass, muddle the lime, 1 mint sprig, and all but a few of the raspberries. Stir in the nonalcoholic white wine, lime juice, and simple syrup. Add ice and top with the seltzer. Garnish with the remaining mint and raspberries for a serene sipper.

SPARKLING NEGRONI

Is it a spritz? Is it a negroni? It's both and it's everything. The Sparkling Negroni features some of the foundational players of those Italian showstoppers and dolls it all up with blood orange. Bask away the rest of your day with a drink that will have you feeling radiant.

Makes 1 mocktail

- 1 ounce nonalcoholic Campari liqueur
- 1 ounce nonalcoholic gin
- 3–4 blood orange slices
- 2 ounces soda water
- 1 thyme sprig

In a glass filled with ice, add the nonalcoholic Campari liqueur and nonalcoholic gin. Give the blood oranges a squeeze before placing them in the glass and top everything off with the soda water. Garnish with the thyme sprig and feel that warm glow of contentment.

NEVER BETTER ICED TEA

Sip away the day with the Never Better Iced Tea. The rejuvenating oolong is a welcome shift away from plain ol' black tea, and the addition of your favorite no-booze spirit—like an herbaceous gin or a smoky whiskey—makes this a feel-good drink that will pull you out of that post-work slump.

Makes 1 mocktail

- 1 oolong tea bag
- ⅔ cup boiling water
- 1 ounce nonalcoholic spirit
- ½ ounce mint simple syrup
- Lime wheels
- 1 mint sprig

Steep the oolong tea in the boiling water for five minutes. Remove the tea bag and refrigerate the liquid to cool completely. In a large glass filled with ice, combine the oolong tea, nonalcoholic spirit, mint simple syrup, and lime wheels. Garnish with the mint sprig and feel refreshed.

♟ BEVS WITH BENEFITS

Ooh, oolong. This ancient wonder is all things healing. It's a great source of magnesium and has been known to improve cognition and sleep, making it a perfect conveyor of calm in your zero-proof recipes.

PRETTY IN PURPLE MARTINI

It's a stunner, a beauty, an elixir all the other mocktails whisper about! The Pretty in Purple Martini is maybe too gorgeous for its own good, and it's not even high-maintenance. Just a quick spin in the cocktail shaker with these transfixing martini ingredients, and you'll have springtime in a glass.

Makes 1 mocktail

- 2½ ounces nonalcoholic gin
- ½ ounce violet syrup
- 1 lavender sprig

In a cocktail shaker filled with ice, combine the nonalcoholic gin and violet syrup. Shake and strain into a martini glass. Garnish with the lavender sprig and fall in love with this drink.

ORANGE-THYME DETOX

It's all about that mocktail glow with the Orange-Thyme Detox. Choose a dry nonalcoholic white wine or aperitif with mood-soothing benefits and make your own simple syrup using the Mocktail Magic on page 24. Let go of what ails you with an herbal concoction that's easy to prepare and easier to imbibe.

Makes 1 mocktail

- 4 ounces nonalcoholic white wine
- 1 ounce thyme simple syrup
- Splash soda water
- 2–3 orange slices
- 1 thyme sprig

In a cocktail glass filled with ice, combine the nonalcoholic white wine, thyme simple syrup, and soda water. Garnish with the orange slices and thyme and savor the aromatherapy.

CHAPTER 3

OH THIS?
IT'S A MOCKTAIL!

Lavender Field
Lemonade.......................... 62

Pumpkin Spice Libation.... 65

Passion Fruit Margarita ... 66

Ritzy Cosmo.......................... 69

Ocean Mister 70

Strawberry Mimosas 73

Watermelon Limeade....... 74

Sex on the Beach................. 77

Pisco Sour 78

Blackberry Spritz................. 81

Grapefruit Grove
Reviver.................................... 82

Hibiscus Sour 85

Spicy Margarita................. 86

Guava Juicer....................... 89

LAVENDER FIELD LEMONADE

Stir up something beautiful! This picturesque purple drink gets its shocking color from butterfly pea flower tea. The tea itself is a cerulean blue that lightens when combined with citrus. If you are using loose-leaf flowers in the recipe below, all you need is one tablespoon. Put on your wide-brimmed sun hat, wander through your nearest lavender field, and enjoy this dazzling lemonade.

Makes 1 mocktail

- 1 butterfly pea flower tea bag
- ½ cup boiling water
- 4 ounces lemon juice
- ¾ ounce lavender simple syrup
- Spritz of lime
- 1 flower sprig

Steep the butterfly pea tea in the boiling water for five minutes. Remove the tea bag and let the liquid cool. In a glass filled with ice, add the lemon juice, lavender simple syrup, and spritz of lime. Pour in the butterfly pea tea, stirring, until it becomes a light lavender color. Garnish with the flower sprig and raise your glass to class.

Bevs with Benefits

Butterfly pea flower can boost your mood, and not just because it's pretty! This magically colorful tea is rich in antioxidant compounds called ternatins, giving it anti-inflammatory properties.

PUMPKIN SPICE LIBATION

Shameless PSL promotion. You can have that Pumpkin Spice Libation whenever you want, and no one here will judge you. A mix of apples, cinnamon, pumpkin, and autumnal joy, this mocktail is a celebration of flavors and is tough to mess up. If you don't have nonalcoholic whiskey or prefer not to use it, swap in apple juice or cider for a sweeter touch.

Makes 1 mocktail

- 1 tablespoon cinnamon sugar
- 2 ounces nonalcoholic whiskey
- 1 tablespoon pumpkin puree
- ¼ teaspoon pumpkin pie spice
- ½ ounce simple syrup
- 2 dashes nonalcoholic bitters
- Spritz of lime
- 2 ounces ginger beer or seltzer

Dampen the rim of a cocktail glass and dip the rim into the cinnamon sugar to coat. Right the glass and fill it with ice. In a cocktail shaker filled with ice, combine the nonalcoholic whiskey, pumpkin puree, pumpkin pie spice, simple syrup, and bitters. Shake well and pour into the prepared glass. Top it off with a spritz of lime and the ginger beer and get cozy with your bevvy.

PASSION FRUIT MARGARITA

Make margaritas and all will be well. With tart and tasty passion fruit as the center of this recipe, there's nothing not to love in this glass. The nonalcoholic tequila mimics the smoky burn of traditional alcohol, but if you'd prefer to forgo it entirely and add more soda water, go right ahead. The passion fruit knows how to show up.

Makes 1 mocktail

- 2 ounces nonalcoholic tequila
- 1½ ounces passion fruit juice
- ½ ounce lime juice
- ½ ounce simple syrup
- Splash soda water
- ½ passion fruit

In a glass filled with ice, combine the nonalcoholic tequila, passion fruit juice, lime juice, simple syrup, and soda water. Scoop a spoonful of the passion fruit into the drink for added texture, or slice off a medallion to use as a garnish.

RITZY COSMO

Sip into something more comfortable with the Ritzy Cosmo. This mocktail takes the regular cosmopolitan and gives it a pleasant fizz, much like a sour, adding an extra layer of depth to this old girl.

Makes 1 mocktail

- 1½ ounces nonalcoholic vodka
- 1½ ounces nonalcoholic orange liqueur
- 1 ounce cranberry juice
- ½ ounce lime juice
- 1 egg white
- 1 dried orange wheel

In a cocktail shaker filled with ice, combine the nonalcoholic vodka, nonalcoholic orange liqueur, cranberry juice, lime juice, and egg white. Shake vigorously for one minute and strain into a coupe glass. Garnish with the dried orange and get sipping.

BEVS WITH BENEFITS

Why use nonalcoholic spirits? It's all in the ritual. Like sugar, the thought of happy hour or that post-work glass of wine triggers the reward center in our brains. With nonalcoholic spirits, we can hear the pop of a cork, the clinking of glassware, and the shake of ice and experience the buzz of a first sip without the aftereffects of alcohol.

OCEAN MISTER

If you hold this drink up to your ear, you can hear the ocean. The Ocean Mister mocktail has depth without being overly complex. Butterfly pea tea gives this drink its striking color, which will remain a dark, mysterious blue so long as no citrus is added. With just a touch of thyme simple syrup, the iced tea transforms into mocktail perfection.

Makes 1 mocktail

- 1 butterfly pea flower tea bag
- ½ cup boiling water
- ½ ounce thyme simple syrup
- 1 thyme sprig

Steep the butterfly pea tea in the boiling water for five minutes. Remove the tea bag and let the liquid cool. In a coupe glass filled with ice, add the butterfly pea tea and the thyme simple syrup. Garnish with the thyme sprig and imagine a cool breeze with every tilt of the glass.

STRAWBERRY MIMOSAS

It's a strawberry party! This mocktail has a sneaky ingredient: guava juice. This killer combo of strawberry and guava makes for a sweet and fun twist on a traditional mimosa. Here's your cue to show Sunday brunch what it's missing.

Makes 6–8 mocktails

• 1½ cups strawberries, stems removed
• 1½ cups pink guava juice
• 1 (750 ml) bottle nonalcoholic sparkling wine
• Halved strawberries

In a blender, combine the strawberries and guava juice and blend until smooth. Strain the mixture through a fine-mesh sieve to remove the extra pulp. In champagne flutes, pour the sparkling wine about halfway to the top and stir in the strawberry-guava blend. Garnish with strawberry halves and enjoy.

 BEVS WITH BENEFITS

Look at these upsides! Drinking nonalcoholic wine has numerous health benefits. The lack of alcohol can mean better sleep, healthy weight loss (alcohol itself is calorie-dense), lower cholesterol, lower blood pressure, and reduced risk of stroke.

WATERMELON LIMEADE

If lemonade is so special, why is lime in everything? Take a moment to celebrate limeade, lemonade's underappreciated sibling that does all the hard work. Pucker up to this zesty duo of watermelon and lime for a delightfully refreshing libation.

Makes 1 mocktail

- 1 cup seedless watermelon cubes
- 1 ounce lime juice
- 1 teaspoon simple syrup
- Splash soda water
- 1 lime wedge

In a blender, combine the watermelon, lime juice, and simple syrup and blend until smooth. Strain the mixture through a fine-mesh sieve to remove the extra pulp. In a glass filled with ice, add the juice and top it off with soda water. Garnish with the lime wedge and kick back.

SEX ON THE BEACH

Mix up an old favorite with an alcohol-free Sex on the Beach. This combination contains all of the same notes as the original, but it's lighter on the sugary juices and nixes the alcohol entirely. Bubbly, sweet, and easily drinkable, it won't mind sticking around for a while.

Makes 1 mocktail

- **2½ ounces peach juice**
- **½ ounce orange juice**
- **2 ounces cranberry seltzer**
- **1 tablespoon pomegranate syrup**
- **2 orange slices**
- **1 maraschino cherry**

In a glass filled with ice, combine the peach juice, orange juice, cranberry seltzer, and pomegranate syrup. Garnish with the orange slices and maraschino cherry for a seaside rendezvous.

PISCO SOUR

It's Pisco Sour hour. Classic pisco comes from fermented grapes, so this version takes its cues from the original and swaps in white grape juice. The tang of lemon cuts some of the sweetness and the egg white makes this nice drink delightfully frothy. When it all comes together, practice your barista skills by transforming the drops of bitters into your very own Mona Lisa.

Makes 1 mocktail

- 2 ounces white grape juice
- 1 ounce lemon juice
- 1 egg white
- 4 dashes nonalcoholic bitters

In a cocktail shaker filled with ice, combine the grape juice, lemon juice, and egg white. Shake vigorously for one minute and strain into a coupe glass. Carefully drop 4 dashes of bitters in a line onto the drink. Glide a toothpick or knife tip through the dots to create a unique design.

BLACKBERRY SPRITZ

There's more to this mocktail than meets the eye. A reviving potion of hydrating liquids and nature's classiest-looking berry, the Blackberry Spritz is an easy go-to with star power. The refreshing combination of blackberry and basil will snap you right out of that workday daze and send you to your happy place.

Makes 1 mocktail

- ½ cup fresh blackberries, divided
- 2 basil leaves
- ½ ounce simple syrup
- ½ ounce lime juice
- 2 ounces coconut water
- 2 ounces soda water

In a cocktail shaker, muddle half of the blackberries, basil, simple syrup, and lime juice. Add the coconut water, then shake and strain into a glass filled with ice. Stir in the soda water and the remaining whole blackberries.

 BEVS WITH BENEFITS

Coconut water makes a great mixer in alcohol-free drinks with a clean, refreshing flavor and a touch of salinity. This unofficial detoxifier is rich in potassium and balances electrolytes, making it great for digestion.

GRAPEFRUIT GROVE REVIVER

Liven up the party with the Grapefruit Grove Reviver. While this drink showcases pink and yellow citrus, the hidden gem is the elderflower syrup. This sugary touch of floral goodness will send you off to a springtime garden with just a whiff from your glass.

Makes 1 mocktail

- 2 ounces pink grapefruit juice
- 1 ounce lemon juice
- 1 ounce elderflower syrup
- 1 flower sprig

In a cocktail shaker filled with ice, combine the grapefruit juice, lemon juice, and elderflower syrup. Shake and strain into a coupe glass. Garnish with the flower sprig and go frolic in a field.

HIBISCUS SOUR

Ooh la la. This gorgeous pink drink has it all. She's perky, she's peppy, and she means business. Shake it all together and you've got yourself one dramatic and lively mocktail.

Makes 1 mocktail

- 1 hibiscus flower tea bag
- ⅓ cup boiling water
- ½ ounce lemon juice
- ½ ounce grapefruit juice
- ½ ounce simple syrup
- 1 egg white
- Hibiscus tea petals

Steep the hibiscus tea in the boiling water for five minutes. Remove the tea bag and refrigerate the liquid to cool completely. In a cocktail shaker filled with ice, combine the hibiscus tea, lemon juice, grapefruit juice, simple syrup, and egg white. Shake vigorously for one minute and strain into a coupe glass. Garnish with the hibiscus petals.

MOCKTAIL MAGIC

Are flower petals glam? Yes. Are they also magic fairy dust? Probably. Both hibiscus petals and butterfly pea petals have color-changing properties. Ever notice how a hibiscus lemonade is bright pink, but the tea is dark red? The magic is in the addition of citrus, which turns the teas from dark concentrated colors to bright pinks and purples.

SPICY MARGARITA

No alcohol = no edge? Try again. This Spicy Margarita won't let you forget it once the glass is empty. The nonalcoholic tequila is here for the mems, but if you want to skip it, you can just add another ounce of lime juice to balance it out.

Makes 1 mocktail

- 1 tablespoon Tajín
- 2 ounces nonalcoholic tequila
- 2 ounces orange juice
- 1 ounce lime juice
- 1 ounce jalapeño simple syrup
- 1 orange wheel
- 1 lime wheel
- 1 mint sprig

Dampen the rim of a cocktail glass and dip the rim into the Tajín to coat. In a cocktail shaker filled with ice, combine the nonalcoholic tequila, orange juice, lime juice, and jalapeño simple syrup. Shake and pour into the glass with ice. Garnish with the orange, lime, and mint.

MOCKTAIL MAGIC ✦

Make your own Tajín at home. Just combine 2 tablespoons chipotle powder, 2 tablespoons ancho chile powder, 2 tablespoons salt, and 4 tablespoons crystallized lime powder. It's the perfect spice mix to garnish drinks or sprinkle on cold fruit like mango or cantaloupe.

GUAVA JUICER

Give guava a little love. As the star of this show, guava surprises and delights with its tangy and sour juice. Add a touch of honey, and it's a refreshing, vitamin-C-packed potion you'll want to keep coming back to.

Makes 1 mocktail

- 1 green guava, seeded and chopped
- 2 ounces water
- 1 ounce honey
- Spritz of lime

In a blender, combine the guava, water, and honey and blend until smooth. If the mixture is too thick, add a little water until it reaches the desired consistency. Strain the mixture through a fine-mesh sieve to remove the extra pulp. In a glass filled with ice, add the juice and spritz it with the lime.

CHAPTER 4

ICY BLENDS
&SWEET TREATS

Mango Lemonade............ 92

Strawberry Daiquiris ... 95

Lychee Slushie.................. 96

Watermelon Coolers......... 99

Matcha Mixer.................100

Italian Ice.........................103

Melon Icers.................... 104

Cherry Daiquiris............. 107

Peach Bellini....................... 108

Yes Way, Frosé 111

Minty Grasshopper...........112

Chocolate Martini............ 115

It's a Party Milkshakes.......116

Frozen Espresso
Martini 119

MANGO LEMONADE

Break out that picnic basket; this icy treat is good for the whole group. Mango Lemonade is where mango shines, but you can adjust the ratio of mango to lemon depending on your preference. Pour this mixture over heaps of crushed ice, and you have yourself a slushie treat.

Makes 6–8 mocktails

- 3 cups cubed mango
- 4 ounces honey simple syrup
- 2 ounces lemon juice
- 4 cups water
- Flower sprigs
- Lime wheels

In a blender, combine the mango, honey simple syrup, lemon juice, and water and blend until smooth. Strain the mixture through a fine-mesh sieve to remove the extra pulp. Serve in large glasses filled with crushed ice. Garnish with the flower sprigs and lime wheels before you relax and watch the clouds go by.

STRAWBERRY DAIQUIRIS

Is that the dulcet tone of a blender in the distance? A racket to the pessimist and the sweet sound of vacation to the optimist, this drink is an icy paradise right in front of you. Follow this recipe closely or do whatever you want—who cares? The Strawberry Daiquiri is your boss now.

Makes 2 mocktails

- 2 cups frozen strawberries
- ½ cup fresh strawberries, stemmed, plus some for garnish
- 2 ounces nonalcoholic rum
- 1½ ounces lime juice
- 2 ounces agave

In a blender, combine the ingredients and blend until smooth. If the mixture is too thick, add a little water until it reaches the desired consistency. Pour into daiquiri glasses and garnish with fresh strawberries for a drink so easy, it'll feel all inclusive.

LYCHEE SLUSHIE

Lychee, you rascal. This playful fruit is patiently waiting for when you've just about had enough of citrus. Smooth, sweet, and almost floral, the soft flavors of this Lychee Slushie are as calming as they are satisfying. The dash of pomegranate syrup gives the slush its hue for a pleasantly pink concoction.

Makes 1 mocktail

- 2½ ounces lychee juice
- 1½ ounces lychee syrup (from the can)
- ½ ounce lime juice
- 1 tablespoon pomegranate syrup
- 1 cup ice
- 2–3 lychee fruit

In a blender, combine the lychee juice, lychee syrup, lime juice, pomegranate syrup, and ice and blend until smooth. Pour into a daiquiri glass, garnish with skewered lychees, and watch all your cares drift away.

WATERMELON COOLERS

Who knew happiness was a frozen watermelon? It's as if this perfect fruit were asking to be blended up into slushie goodness. With a smidge of this and a spritz of that, you'll have yourself a Watermelon Cooler that refreshes, revives, and satisfies.

Makes 4 mocktails

- 10 cups frozen seedless watermelon cubes
- 2 tablespoons maple syrup
- 8 ounces water
- Juice of 1 lime
- ¼ cup fresh mint, plus 4 sprigs for garnish
- 4 watermelon slices

In a blender, combine the watermelon cubes, maple syrup, water, lime juice, and mint and blend until smooth. If the mixture is too thick, add a little water until it reaches the desired consistency. Pour into large glasses, garnish with the watermelon slices and mint sprigs, and find yourself a picnic.

MATCHA MIXER

Meet your matcha! Smooth enough to perk you up and sweet enough to be a dessert, the Matcha Mixer can hold its own wherever it's poured. There's a little extra satisfaction knowing that something this tasty has all the benefits of green tea!

Makes 1 mocktail

- 1 teaspoon matcha powder
- 1 tablespoon hot water
- 2 ounces warm water
- 4 ounces milk of choice
- ½ ounce simple syrup

In a small bowl, whisk the matcha powder and 1 tablespoon hot water together. Stir in the warm water and transfer to the refrigerator to cool. In a glass filled with ice, combine the matcha liquid, milk, and simple syrup.

BEVS WITH BENEFITS

Matcha sure is pretty, but it's not all about looks. Made from ground green tea leaves, matcha is high in antioxidants like catechins, which are associated with good heart health. Matcha is a great alternative to coffee for sustained energy without all the jitters, and you can enjoy it hot, chilled, or as the star ingredient in sweet treats.

ITALIAN ICE

Break out that umbrella, here's a citrusy slushie that feels like a beach day—no long lines required. Choose a nonalcoholic spirit with a refreshing zip, like a replacement gin, and adjust the level of citrus and sweetness depending on your palate.

Makes 2 mocktails

- 1 ounce nonalcoholic spirit
- Juice of 1 lime
- 2 ounces mint simple syrup
- 1½ cups ice
- 2 lime wheels
- 2 mint sprigs

In a blender, combine the nonalcoholic spirit, lime juice, simple syrup, and ice and blend until smooth. If the mixture is too thick, add a little water until it reaches the desired consistency. Pour into large glasses and garnish with lime and mint for a bright and zesty sip of sunshine.

MELON ICERS

Oh, honey. The Melon Icer gets to give golden honeydew the stage it deserves. This humble fruit is softly sugary, making for a crisp slush that cools you down without hitting you in the face with its sweetness.

Makes 2–4 mocktails

- 1 golden honeydew melon, seeded, peeled, and chopped
- 2 ounces water
- 1 ounce honey
- Spritz of lime
- 2-4 mint sprigs

In a blender, combine all but a couple of slices of the melon, water, and honey and blend until smooth. If the mixture is too thick, add a little water until it reaches the desired consistency. Strain the mixture through a fine-mesh sieve to remove the extra pulp. In glasses filled with crushed ice, add the juice and spritz it with the lime. Decorate with the melon slices and mint sprigs.

MOCKTAIL MAGIC

Do you have a juicer? Use it for recipes like this that would otherwise require straining and a touch of upper-arm strength.

CHERRY DAIQUIRIS

Good choices come with a cherry on top. Blend up this ruby-red Cherry Daiquiri for a little something nourishing. Perfect as a dessert or as a present to yourself, this chilly mix of juice and fruit is bright, tart, and never boring.

Makes 2 mocktails

- 8 ounces cranberry juice
- 1 cup frozen cherries
- 1 frozen banana, peeled
- ½ ounce honey
- ½ cup fresh cherries, sliced
- 2 mint sprigs

In a blender, combine the cranberry juice, frozen cherries, banana, and honey and blend until smooth. If the mixture is too thick, add a little water until it reaches the desired consistency. Pour into glasses and garnish with fresh cherries and mint for a peppy little something.

PEACH BELLINI

Make it a Bellini day. This Peach Bellini has a surprise twist (it's mango). A perfect duo of tart and sweet with the sparkle of your favorite bubbles, this pleasant drink is zippy, refreshing, and feels like a day off.

Makes 1 mocktail

- **4 ounces nonalcoholic prosecco**
- **1 ounce peach puree**
- **1 ounce mango puree**
- **1 peach slice**

In a cocktail shaker, stir the nonalcohlic prosecco, peach puree, and mango puree until combined. Pour the mixture into a martini glass filled with crushed ice. Garnish with a peach slice and enjoy your adult slushie.

YES WAY, FROSÉ

This one's for the squad. Yes Way, Frosé is a perfect excuse for revelry in a glass. Choose a nonalcoholic rosé that's nice and dry so the frosé isn't overly sweet, and you will know true joy. Blend this up for literally any reason.

Makes 6–8 mocktails

- 1 (750 ml) bottle nonalcoholic rosé
- 1 cup strawberries, stems removed
- Juice of 1 lemon
- ½ cup honey

Pour the nonalcoholic rosé into an ice cube tray, reserving 1 cup of rosé in the refrigerator for later. Freeze overnight or for at least four hours until the cubes are completely frozen. In a blender, combine the rosé cubes, strawberries, lemon juice, honey, and 1 cup of reserved rosé and blend until slushie. Pour into cocktail glasses and laze away.

 BEVS WITH BENEFITS

You can have "rosé all day" and feel great about it with nonalcoholic wines. These zero-proof wonders do their part to reduce stress, maintain healthy blood pressure, and keep you feeling relaxed.

MINTY GRASSHOPPER

Take an old drink but make it cute. This Minty Grasshopper is all glam, and probably because it was invented just ahead of the roaring (nineteen) twenties. This version makes good use of nonalcoholic liqueurs for a note-for-note replica.

Makes 1 mocktail

- 1 ounce nonalcoholic green crème de menthe
- 1 ounce nonalcoholic clear crème de cacao
- 1 ounce heavy cream
- 1 mint sprig

In a cocktail shaker filled with ice, combine the nonalcoholic crème de menthe, crème de cacao, and heavy cream. Shake and strain into a coupe glass. Garnish with a mint sprig and hop into a sweet treat.

CHOCOLATE MARTINI

As if chocolate needed a reason to be elevated, this Chocolate Martini is all class. An understated yet perfect amount of cocoa flavor, this blend of liquids is a dreamy elixir for chocolate lovers everywhere.

Makes 1 mocktail

- 1 ounce nonalcoholic chocolate liqueur
- 1 ounce nonalcoholic crème de cacao
- 1 ounce nonalcoholic spirit
- ½ ounce half-and-half
- 2 rosemary sprigs
- Shaved nutmeg

In a cocktail shaker filled with ice, combine the nonalcoholic chocolate liqueur, nonalcoholic crème de cacao, nonalcoholic spirit, half-and-half, and 1 rosemary sprig. Shake and strain into a coupe glass. Garnish with the other rosemary sprig and a sprinkle of nutmeg, and savor this sippable touch of dessert.

MOCKTAIL MAGIC ✦

Want to wow? Give your mocktails a little pyrotechnic twist. Before garnishing this drink, carefully burn the ends of the rosemary to bring out its aroma. Waft the smoke around the drink, blow out the flame, and garnish accordingly. The lingering scent will feel cozy and festive.

IT'S A PARTY MILKSHAKES

Choose chaos—it's a party! Celebrate decadence with a special treat that will bring a smile to your face, no matter how long it'll take for you to stop finding sprinkles everywhere.

Makes 2 mocktails

- 1 tablespoon chocolate sauce
- ¼ cup sprinkles
- 2 cups coconut or vanilla ice cream
- ¾ cup milk of choice
- ½ cup white cake mix
- Whipped cream

Line the rim of large glasses with chocolate sauce and dip them in the sprinkles. In a blender, combine the ice cream, milk, and cake mix and blend until smooth. Pour into the sprinkles-lined glasses. Top with whipped cream and additional sprinkles and have yourself a party.

FROZEN ESPRESSO MARTINI

Which drink always comes back into vogue? Joy in a glass. This take on an espresso martini is glamorous as always and contains the elixir of life—cold brew. It's a showstopper, and it'll keep you caffeinated for the foreseeable future.

Makes 1 mocktail

- 2 ounces cold brew concentrate
- 1½ ounces nonalcoholic spirit
- ½ ounce simple syrup
- 1 cup ice
- 3 espresso beans

In a blender, combine the cold brew concentrate, nonalcoholic spirit, simple syrup, and ice and blend until smooth. Pour into a coupe glass, garnish with espresso beans, and feel the pleasant shiver of glorious caffeine.

INDEX

A

Adaptogens, 42, 45
Aloe Vera
    Honeydew-Aloe Cooler, 4
Apple
    Apple Mimosa, 20
Apricot
    Apricot Seltzer, 16

B

Blackberry
    Blackberry Spritz, 81
Blueberries
    Kiwi Summer Water, 12
Butterfly Pea Tea, 85
    Lavender Field Lemonade, 62
    Ocean Mister, 70

C

Campari (nonalcoholic)
    Orange Spritz, 7
    Sparkling Negroni, 53
Chamomile
    Chamomile-Citrus Relaxer, 38
Cherry
    Cherry Daiquiri, 107
Coconut
    Pineapple Sour, 27

Coconut Water
    Blackberry Spritz, 81
Cosmo
    Ritzy Cosmo, 69
Cranberry
    Cherry Daiquiri, 107
    Lavender Cape Codder, 15
    Ritzy Cosmo, 69
    Sex on the Beach, 77
Crème de Cacao (nonalcoholic)
    Chocolate Martini, 115
    Minty Grasshopper, 112
Crème de Menthe (nonalcoholic)
    Minty Grasshopper, 112
Cucumber
    Honeydew-Aloe Cooler, 4

D

Daiquiri
    Cherry Daiquiri, 107
    Strawberry Daiquiri, 95

E

Elderflower
    Grapefruit Grove Reviver, 82

Espresso
    Frozen Espresso Martini, 119
    Sunlit Café Tónica, 8

F

Fig
    Fig Lemonade, 37

G

Gin (nonalcoholic)
    Pretty in Purple Martini, 57
    Sparkling Negroni, 53
Golden Berry
    Golden Berry Spritzer, 42
Grapefruit
    Grapefruit Grove Reviver, 82
    Hibiscus Sour, 85
Grape (white)
    Pisco Sour, 78
Guava
    Guava Juicer, 89
    Strawberry Mimosa, 73

H

Hibiscus
    Hibiscus Iced Tea, 49

Hibiscus Sour, 85
Honeydew Melon
Honeydew-Aloe
Cooler, 4
Melon Icer, 104

J

Ice Cream
It's a Party Milkshake,
116
Iced Tea
Hibiscus Iced Tea, 49
Never Better Iced
Tea, 54

K

Kiwi
Kiwi Summer Water, 12

L

Lavender
Lavender Cape
Codder, 15
Lavender Field
Lemonade, 62
Lemon
Chamomile-Citrus
Relaxer, 38
Lemon Sparkler, 28
Pisco Sour, 78
Pomegranate Spritzer,
23
Lemonade
Fig Lemonade, 37
Lavender Field
Lemonade, 62
Mango Lemonade, 92
Lemon Balm, 42
Lime
Italian Ice, 103

Raspberry Seltzer, 50
Watermelon Mojito, 24
Limeade
Watermelon Limeade,
74
Lychee
Lychee Slushie, 96

M

Mango
Mango Lemonade, 92
Peach Bellini, 108
Maple Syrup
Watermelon Cooler, 99
Margarita
Passion Fruit
Margarita, 66
Spicy Margarita, 86
Martini
Chocolate Martini, 115
Frozen Espresso
Martini, 119
Pretty in Purple
Martini, 57
Matcha
Matcha Mixer, 100
Milk
It's a Party
Milkshake, 116
Mimosa
Apple Mimosa, 20
Strawberry Mimosa, 73
Mint
Italian Ice, 103
Lemon Sparkler, 28
Minty Grasshopper, 112
Orange Mojito, 46
Mojito
Orange Mojito, 46
Watermelon Mojito, 24

O

Oolong Tea
Never Better Iced Tea,
54
Orange
Blood-Orange Zester,
31
Orange Mojito, 46
Orange Spritz, 7
Orange-Thyme Detox,
58
Sex on the Beach, 77
Sparkling Negroni, 53
Spicy Margarita, 86
Orange Liqueur
(nonalcoholic)
Orange Mojito, 46
Ritzy Cosmo, 69

P

Passion Fruit
Passion Fruit
Margarita, 66
Peach
Peach Bellini, 100
Sex on the Beach, 77
Pear
Pear & Cinnamon
Sparkler, 44
Pineapple
Pineapple Sour, 27
Pomegranate
Lychee Slushie, 96
Pomegranate Glimmer,
41
Pomegranate Spritzer,
23
Pumpkin
Pumpkin Spice
Libation, 65

R

Raspberry
    Raspberry Seltzer, 50
Rosé (nonalcoholic)
    Yes Way, Frosé, 111
Rose Water
    Rose Water Garden
        Party, 34
    Strawberry Water, 19

S

Seltzer
    Apricot Seltzer, 16
    Raspberry Seltzer, 50
Simple Syrup, 24
Sour
    Hibiscus Sour, 85
    Pineapple Sour, 27
    Pisco Sour, 78
Spritz
    Blackberry Spritz, 81
    Orange Spritz, 7
    Summer in Italy Spritz,
        11
Spritzer
    Golden Berry Spritzer,
        42
    Pomegranate Spritzer,
        23
Strawberry
    Strawberry Daiquiri, 95
    Strawberry Mimosa, 73
    Strawberry Water, 19
    Yes Way, Frosé, 111

T

Tajin
    Spicy Margarita, 86
Tequila (nonalcoholic)
    Passion Fruit
        Margarita, 66
    Spicy Margarita, 86
    L-Theanine, 42

Thyme
    Ocean Mister, 70
    Orange-Thyme
        Detox, 58

V

Violet Syrup
    Pretty in Purple
        Martini, 57
Vodka (nonalcoholic)
    Ritzy Cosmo, 69

W

Watermelon
    Watermelon Cooler, 99
    Watermelon Limeade,
        74
    Watermelon Mojito, 24